USING THIS BOOK

*One of the best ways of helping children to learn to read is by reading stories to them and with them. This way they learn what **reading** is, and* they will gradually come to recognise many words, and begin to read for themselves.

First, grown-ups read the story on the left-hand pages aloud to the child.

You can reread the story as often as the child enjoys hearing it. Talk about the pictures as you go.

Later the child is encouraged to read the words under the pictures on the right-hand page.

The pages at the back of the book will give you some ideas for helping your child to read.

British Library Cataloguing in Publication Data
McCullagh, Sheila K.
    Toby Spelldragon and the magician.
    (Puddle lane. Stage 1; 15)
    1. Readers—*1950-*
    I. Title   II. Davis, Jon   III. Series
    428.6   PE1119
    ISBN 0-7214-1008-1

First edition

Published by Ladybird Books Ltd Loughborough Leicestershire UK
Ladybird Books Inc Lewiston Maine 04240 USA

© Text and layout SHEILA McCULLAGH MCMLXXXVI
© In publication LADYBIRD BOOKS LTD MCMLXXXVI
Toby Spelldragon © ♥ YORKSHIRE TELEVISION LIMITED MCMLXXXV
All rights reserved. No part of this publication may be reproduced, stored in a retrieval system, or transmitted in any form or by any means, electronic, mechanical, photo-copying, recording or otherwise, without the prior consent of the copyright owners.

Printed in England

Toby Spelldragon and the Magician

written by SHEILA McCULLAGH
illustrated by JON DAVIS

This book belongs to:

poisy

Ladybird Books

One day, Toby Spelldragon
was sitting at the window
of the Magician's room,
looking down into the garden.
He was watching three little mice.
Two of the mice, Jeremy and Miranda,
were chasing each other
around and up and over
an upturned flowerpot.
Chestnut Mouse was sitting on a stone,
watching them.

Toby Spelldragon

Jeremy and Miranda
were so busy playing,
that they didn't see Tom Cat.
But Tom Cat saw them.
He was crouching in Puddle Lane,
looking in through the gates.
He could see Jeremy and Miranda
every time they climbed up
onto the flowerpot.

Tom Cat saw
Jeremy and Miranda.

Very softly, Tom Cat crept
under the gate, and into the garden.
He crept nearer and nearer
to the three little mice.
He twitched his tail.
Chestnut saw his tail move.
He shouted a warning,
and dived into a hole
near the stone.

Chestnut shouted.

Jeremy and Miranda didn't wait
to see what Chestnut
was warning them about.
They dived down into the flowerpot
through the hole in the top,
and hid.

Jeremy and
Miranda hid.

Tom Cat reached the flowerpot.
He walked slowly all around it,
sniffing as he went.
He could smell mice, and
he could hear mice.
He stood up, put his front paws
on the top of the flowerpot,
and looked down the hole.

Tom Cat looked
down the hole.

Toby Spelldragon hurried across
the Magician's room, and
climbed up onto the table.
The Magician was sitting there,
writing a book about magic.
He had just got to
a very difficult spell, and
he was writing first with a green pen,
and then with a red pen.

Toby went
to the Magician.

"Stop writing!" said Toby.
"You've got to do something.
Tom Cat is in the garden."

"Go away and don't bother me,"
said the Magician.
"I haven't finished this yet."

"But Tom Cat is after the mice,"
said Toby.

"The mice can look after themselves,"
said the Magician.
"They're much cleverer than Tom Cat."
And he went on writing.

"Go away!"
said the Magician.

Toby muttered a spell,
and twitched his tail.
The Magician's red pen
vanished out of his hand.
The Magician looked up.
"Toby!" he said.
"Where's my red pen?"

"I haven't got it," said Toby.
"Come and look out of the window."

The Magician's red pen
vanished.

"I will in a few minutes,"
said the Magician. "But
I want to finish this first."
He turned back to his book.
His green pen had vanished.
"Toby!" said the Magician,
"I **must** finish this, or
I shall forget what I'm writing."

"You can have your old pens, then,"
said Toby.
The red and green pens reappeared
on the table, but the book vanished.

The Magician's book
vanished.

"Toby!" said the Magician firmly.
He pushed back his chair,
and stood up.

"Come to the window!" said Toby.
"Tom Cat is trying to eat
Jeremy and Miranda."

"What!" exclaimed the Magician.
He ran to the window.

"I've been trying to tell you,
but you wouldn't listen,"
said Toby.

The Magician
ran to the window.

The Magician looked down
into the garden.
Tom Cat had just discovered
that he could rock the flowerpot
to and fro.

The Magician
looked down.

There wasn't time for a spell.
The Magician seized a horn
that was hanging on the wall.
He leaned out of the window,
and blew it.
"What good will that do?" said Toby.
"It will take more than that
to scare Tom Cat."

"I'm calling the Gruffle,"
said the Magician.
"The Gruffle hates cats."

(The Gruffle was a red monster.
He was very gruff and grumpy,
and he could vanish
when he wanted to.)

The Magician blew.

At that moment, the Gruffle arrived.
He came rushing around
the corner of the house,
breathing out fire and smoke.
He saw Tom Cat by the flowerpot,
and he roared in fury.
A great puff of fire and smoke
shot out of the Gruffle's mouth
towards Tom Cat.

the Gruffle

Tom Cat was so frightened
at the sight of the Gruffle,
that for one second he stayed
standing by the flowerpot,
too frightened to move.
Then he leapt sideways,
and ran away.
He fled towards the gates,
with the Gruffle after him.

Tom Cat ran away.

He got to the gate
just in time.
He shot underneath it
like a bullet from a gun.
He rushed away down Puddle Lane
as fast as he could run.

Tom Cat ran
down Puddle Lane.

The Gruffle stopped at the gate,
and peered down Puddle Lane.

He couldn't run very fast,
and Tom Cat was disappearing
into the distance.
The Gruffle shot a puff
of fire and smoke through the gate,
and came back into the garden.

The Gruffle
came back
into the garden.

Jeremy and Miranda were standing
on top of the flowerpot,
wondering if it was safe
to run home.
The Gruffle saw them.

The Gruffle saw
Jeremy and Miranda.

The Gruffle gave a great roar,
and vanished.
"Where has the Gruffle gone?"
asked Toby. (He was still
watching from the window.)

"I expect he's gone back
to the old castle,"
said the Magician.
"He's afraid of mice."

"Afraid of mice?" cried Toby.
"Don't tell that to Tom Cat!"
He began to laugh.
Jeremy and Miranda
ran back to the hollow tree.

The Gruffle vanished.
Jeremy and Miranda
ran home.

"And now perhaps you'll let me
finish my work," said the Magician.

"I'm not stopping you writing,"
said Toby. "Not now.
I'll come and help you."

"Please don't!" said the Magician.
"At least, not yet.
You can help me soon."

He went back to the table.
The book and the green and red pens
were all there.
The Magician sat down, and
began to write.

The Magician
sat down again.

Notes for the parent/teacher

When you have read the story, go back to the beginning. Look at each picture and talk about it, pointing to the caption below, and reading it aloud yourself.

Run your finger along under the words as you read, so that the child learns that reading goes from left to right. (You needn't say this in so many words. Children learn many useful things about reading by just reading with you, and it is often better to let them learn by experience, rather than by explanation.) When you next go through the book, encourage the child to read the words and sentences under the illustrations.

"Do you live here?" asked Jeremy.
"No," said Chestnut.
"I live in the Magician's garden,
at the end of Puddle Lane.
But I always come here on Fridays.
They have cheese and nuts
in the market on Fridays.
Come and see."
Jeremy looked down.
He looked at one of the tables.
There was a big cheese
at one end of the table,
and a basket of nuts
at the other end.

Jeremy looked down.

Don't rush in with the word before he* has time to think, but don't leave him struggling for too long. Always encourage him to feel that he is reading successfully, praising him when he does well, and avoiding criticism.

Now turn back to the beginning, and print the child's name in the space on the title page, using ordinary, not capital letters. Let him watch you print it: this is another useful experience.

*Children enjoy hearing the same story many times. Read this one as often as the child likes hearing it. The more opportunities he has of looking at the illustrations and **reading** the captions with you, the more he will come to recognise the words. Don't worry if he **remembers** rather than **reads** the captions. This is a normal stage in learning.*

If you have a number of books, let him choose which story he would like to have again.

---

*Footnote: In order to avoid the continual "she or he", "her or him", the child is referred to in this book as "he". However, the stories are equally appropriate for girls and boys.

Have you read these stories from Stage 1 about Tom Cat and the mice?

Stage 1

from
Jeremy Mouse
and Mr Puffle

from Tom Cat and the
Wideawake Mice